Listening to Children in their Early Years

by
Dr Hannah Mortimer
with SureStart Stockton-on-Tees

Illustrated by
Robyn Gallow

Acknowledgement
The staff and children of Hartburn Primary School,
High Flyers Early Support Nursery and Footsteps Nursery, Billingham

A QEd Publication

Published in 2007

ISBN 978 1 898873 52 5

British Library Cataloguing
A catalogue record for this book is available from the British Library.

Published by QEd Publications, 39 Weeping Cross, Stafford ST17 0DG
Tel: 01785 620364
Fax: 01785 607797
Web site: www.qed.uk.com
Email: orders@qed.uk.com

Printed by Gutenberg Press Ltd, Malta.

Contents

Introduction

The aim of the book

This book could have had any number of titles. *Listening to Children in their Early Years* was selected out of all of those considered because it was the most child-centred. However, 'listening' is used in its widest sense and involves tuning into children, seeing the world from their own points of view, offering them choices, consulting them on matters that are important to their lives and adjusting what we do in the light of their responses. In other words, the process of 'listening' should involve all our senses as we take active steps to encourage each and every child's participation and belonging.

Listening to children has been defined as:

- An active process of receiving, interpreting and responding to communication. It includes all the senses and emotions and is not limited to the spoken word.

- A necessary stage in ensuring the participation of all children.

- An ongoing part of tuning in to all children as individuals in their everyday lives.

- Sometimes part of a specific consultation about a particular environment, choice, event or opportunity.

from Listening as a way of life (National Children's Bureau)

We can sum these up as:
- **Communicating effectively.**
- **Encouraging participation.**
- **Tuning in.**
- **Offering choices.**

In this book, you will find chapters on each of these processes with some further chapters on interesting projects that you might like to try yourselves.

An Early Years Participation Project, Stockton-on-Tees

During 2006/7, the author was given the brief to 'work up' the document 'Consulting with children in the Early Years' into an approach that could be celebrated, shared and delivered as training in Stockton-on-Tees Borough. The project focused on *how* early years teachers and practitioners can consult with even very young children under five.

The specific aims of the project were:

- To develop and then collect examples of good practice within three diverse settings: a foundation class in a primary school, a SureStart children's centre nursery and an early support nursery.

- To build these into a training package and materials that could be delivered to early years staff.

This book and the training that accompanied it are the result of that work. You can read all about the good practice examples in Chapters 6 to 8 on 'Babywatch', 'A Children's Prospectus' and 'Friendship Matters'.

Who the book is aimed at

This book is for everyone living and working with young children from birth to five. It will be useful for early years educators working in all kinds of early years settings: Early Years Foundation Stage (EYFS) classes within schools, non-maintained early years settings, playgroups, children's centres, pre-schools, private nurseries, day nurseries, at the childminder's and crèches. It will also be helpful for individuals training on NVQ or early childhood courses and of interest to parents and carers of children in their early years.

Chapter One

Listening to, consulting and participating with young children

All the best journeys start with a vision either about where you want to go – or at least the way you would like to travel and the luggage you will take with you. In this chapter, we explore the values and vision that guide us when setting out to listen to, involve and consult with each and every child in an early years setting. This is what we might aim for.

The basic belief

Young children have a right to have their views taken into account when we plan and deliver our early years provision on:

- equal opportunity grounds because they are part of our community;

- educational grounds so we can better match activity and learner;

- psychological grounds because we know that active involvement in play, care and learning increases success and well-being.

If you hold the vision that all young children will be 'listened to' in whatever way is possible for them to communicate, then try to think for a moment about what children's voices might tell us if this works in reality. Imagine that these children are speaking about their early years setting. Hold on to these voices to help you in your day-to-day 'listening' to the children.

What I think about my setting

Adults ask me what I would like to do next

Adults listen to me

All children my age can come to this group if they want

The adults help each other too

I know who to go to if I
am not happy here

Children like coming here

I can have a go
at everything

There are lots of
different things to do

My Mum/Dad/parents/
carers are fully involved
in what I do here

Sometimes I like to play alone

The adults are nice and
friendly

We think play and work are
the same things

There is more
than one adult
to help me

Sometimes I work and
play with other children

The adults show you what to
do if you don't know.

They make my family and me
feel welcome

Adapted from Booth et al (2000)

Why listen to children?

We listen to young children because they have a *right* to be heard. The United Nations Convention on the Rights of the Child (1989) Article 12 stated that children who are capable of forming their own views have the right to express those views freely in all matters affecting them, the views of the children being given due weight in accordance with their age and maturity. If we are to allow young children the same equality of opportunity as older people, then we must listen to what their voices, feelings and behaviour are telling us.

We also listen to young children because they have a legal entitlement to be consulted. The Children Act (2000) gave children in Britain a legal right to be consulted on decisions affecting their futures and placement in public care. The Children Act (2004) places a duty on us to work together to promote the well-being of children relating to five outcomes which were chosen in consultation with children:

- be healthy;
- stay safe;
- enjoy and achieve;
- make a positive contribution to society;
- achieve economic well-being.

Underpinning the *Every Child Matters* framework is the notion that children are integral stakeholders in their own learning, social and health care. In order to plan effective services we need to take their views into account as well as other people's. You will read about some ways of doing this in Chapter 5.

Knowing how successful we have been in our delivery of the EYFS involves seeking feedback from the children and families concerned. Another reason, therefore, for listening to young children is because they make better progress if they are fully involved. Children carry important and relevant information about their likes, dislikes, strengths and needs. Their support is crucial to the effective implementation of any intervention. We can better match the opportunities we provide to the children's level of play and development if we provide them with real choices and adapt what we do in light of their decisions. Children's self confidence, self-esteem and mental health are linked to their ability to make choices, take risks in their discovery, initiate play and achieve success. The *SEN Code of Practice* (2001) makes it clear that staff in Government registered settings must look for ways of involving children with special educational needs in the planning and intervention.

How we can listen to young children

In this book you will read about many ways in which you can listen to and consult with young children. Here is a general overview of some of the approaches covered.

Know each as an individual

We can listen to young children by getting to *know each of them as an individual*. Children are more likely to communicate their needs, opinions and feelings to us if we have already established a relationship with them. We are also better able to interpret what they are telling us if we know them well. We understand that children tell us things in many different ways – through their voices, but also through the way they behave and the feelings they express. There are examples to help you 'tune in' to young children in Chapter 4. You will also read about how you can tune into even the youngest children as individuals in Chapter 6 on 'Babywatch'.

Establish likes and dislikes

We can also listen to children by *establishing their likes and dislikes*. We can do this simply by:
- observing children at play;
- offering choices and noting children's selections;
- asking the children to record what they like and dislike on camera;
- talking together in groups;
- using simple questionnaires;
- using one-to-one conversations.

We could also gather information about children's likes, dislikes and how they make their needs known on entry into a service or setting using a simple 'Welcome profile' to gather information (page 20). For children who have special educational needs (SEN) or disability, this becomes especially important. You will find an example of a simple 'Child passport' on page 19 in which new carers are helped to interpret a child's feelings from their expressions and behaviour and to respond accordingly.

Art and crafts

We can listen to young children through their *art and craft work*. We do this by giving them chances to draw and paint and to talk to us about what they are doing. Children's drawings can be talked about together and used to find out about a child's interests and feelings. Sometimes when children have strong feelings or memories, they try to express these through their paintings – by talking to them about their creations, we give them a chance to talk about their feelings too. We usually date the drawing and add any comments the child has made on the back. Musical interactions too can be used to encourage young children to express their feelings. Coram Family Children's Centre has developed an innovative and comprehensive resource for listening to and working with young children so that they can really participate in matters that affect their lives. Using the arts, they enable children under 8 to express views and feelings and help parents and practitioners relate to young children. The resource is called *Listening to Young Children* (Lancaster & Broadbent, 2003).

Using photographs

We can find out what is important to children by using *child-held cameras*. Adults can obtain a child's-eye view of nursery life by providing a camera and encouraging a child to take photographs of the things that are important to him or her. Practitioners can then piece together a picture of children's priorities and impressions by collating evidence from the children themselves and adding the views of parents and nursery colleagues. These can be built into a book or portfolio that can serve as a record of the child's achievements for the future. You will read about this in Chapter 7 on 'A Children's Prospectus' and 'The Mosaic Approach' on page 21.

Stories and pictures

We can use *stories and picture books* as a means of introducing situations and encouraging talking. Early years settings often build up useful collections of stimulus books for covering a range of new situations the child might meet – going to hospital, having a new baby in the family, living with one parent. We can also use picture books to introduce disability and diversity and look for books that portray images of diversity in natural, everyday contexts. There are some suggestions for children's books which encourage talking about feelings listed on page 44.

Imaginative play

We can encourage imaginative play as a means of introducing situations and encouraging talking. For example, when we are planning adaptations and developments that will directly affect the children, we will look for ways of creating these through the small world play and role play that we offer. For example, a new outdoor play area might trigger creating a miniature version in the sand tray or experimenting with new ideas out of doors. Only when children have an idea of 'what's on the menu' will they be able to make informed choices and express preferences. In a similar way, we will use themed play to create new experiences for children (such as going into hospital, for example) so that they have a chance to share their feelings.

Diversity

By providing toys, resources and picture books that reflect diversity we allow children to participate and express themselves. Listening to what children have to say on equality issues shows us that even the youngest children in our settings start to learn about what is different, as well as what is similar, between people. They begin to form values and responses to these differences by observing other people's behaviour and can be sensitive to how children are included or excluded. Children are more likely to feel included and to make their voices known if practitioners make sure that the teaching materials and books within the early years setting reflect a wide range of ability, ethnicity, and culture. Picture books which contain 'models' of differently-abled children can act as talking points. We also need to make sure that the activities we provide, our language and our attitudes, do not promote gender stereotypes.

Assessments

We can involve children in their own on-going EYFS assessments and monitoring by making sure that the assessments we use in our settings are child-centred and play-based. Assessment should arise naturally from familiar situations in which the child is enabled to show off his or her best, as well as the level of need. This is most likely to happen in spontaneous play arising from the opportunities that have been set up in the early years setting, rather than the practitioner isolating a child for 'special testing'. By observing how the child plays naturally, we are 'listening' to their play and behaviour and allowing them to lead.

Planning

We can ensure better participation if we involve the children in our EYFS planning. Are there aspects of the curriculum that children seem less keen on participating in? What aspects of the curriculum do children enjoy most? Why? Can we learn from this in order to make other aspects of our EYFS experiences more appealing to the children? Are there areas of the nursery that are underused? What do the children say about this? Again, what can we learn from this? You will find some examples of how you can answer these questions, perhaps using photography, child conferencing or observations, in Chapter 3.

Special educational needs

For children who have SEN, we can involve them more fully by consulting them about their Individual Education Plans (IEPs). Take a moment to consider the points at which children could be offered choices or asked for their views during a busy session. These can range from simple choices about where, how and who to play with through to what they need to learn next and how to go about it. Practitioners should use their knowledge of the individual children to ask or establish how they feel about their individual education plan, whether they feel comfortable with it, and how they would like to contribute. Make sure, when you are planning additional support, that you do not deny a child the opportunity to play with other children and to learn from each other. You will read more about this in Chapter 8 on 'Friendship Matters'.

Play

We can also listen to children by making sure that *all* children can make *real choices in their play*. Offering choices allows children to direct their own play, provided that practitioners have thought ahead and planned suitable and enjoyable learning experiences for the menu. If a child has additional needs, then we need to make sure that there are 'real' choices on offer by removing any barriers to learning and play. For example, if a child cannot use words to communicate, actual playthings and activities can be offered for the child to select between. Symbols, pictures and objects of reference, such as a spade to suggest sand play or a cup to suggest drinks time, can also be used to encourage a pointing, an eye glance or a yes/no response. There are more examples in Chapter 5.

Monitoring success

How will we know how successful we have been in encouraging children to participate and be consulted? We can do this by regularly observing children's choices and acting on them. Aim to provide play experiences that reflect the children's interests and strengths. If children are opting to avoid a play activity that is an important aspect of the curriculum, then redesign it to be of greater interest and relevance for them. You can also use observations to monitor children's choices, for example using tracking and spider's web observations. There are suggestions for making observations in *The Observation and Assessment of Children in the Early Years* (Mortimer, 2001). The observations and records that you keep should provide evidence that you have not only collected information about the children's choices, but acted on these as well where appropriate.

You can also monitor how effective you are being in your day-to-day listening to children by talking regularly with children in small groups or during circle time and recording what they tell you. Use each child's individual record to add notes on their views, choices of play and what they have told you about their experiences in the setting. Make sure you include sections in all your policy documents about how you consult with children and how children view your early years provision. Each year, you might produce a child's-eye view of your setting, based on evidence you have gathered from the children. These could form sections within your existing policy documents – for example in your Inclusion Policy and your Behaviour Policy. Always record the sources of any evidence so that you can show how your planning was done in the light of feedback from the children. This way, you will be shown to have put the visions and values that we met at the beginning of the chapter into practice.

Chapter Two

Communicating is a two-way process

Listening as a way of life

Listening to young children is an integral part of understanding what they are feeling and what it is they need from their early years experience. As such, it cannot be 'tagged on' to what we do simply by trying an exercise in circle time or sending out a questionnaire to parents and carers. Instead, it should form part of our working lives and flow from the basic beliefs and vision that we hold. The National Children's Bureau has produced a really helpful series of leaflets, all downloadable from their website (see page 42). The series is called *Listening as a way of life* and there are leaflets on why we should listen; supporting parents to listen; listening to babies; listening to children's food preferences; listening to young disabled children; and finding out about what children think about equality issues.

RAMPS

Penny Lancaster has developed a framework for listening to children known as 'RAMPS'. This stands for:

- **R**ecognising children's many languages.
- **A**llocating communication spaces.
- **M**aking time.
- **P**roviding choice.
- **S**ubscribing to a reflective practice.

These principles provide a sound framework to empower children in participatory processes and are embodied in the Coram Family's Listening to Young Children project (see page 43). RAMPS also provides a useful framework for evaluating your professional practice. To help you do this, there is a useful paper *RAMPS: a framework for listening to children* by Penny Lancaster, downloadable from the Daycare Trust (www.daycaretrust.org.uk).

Children's stories

There is some fascinating research carried out through the Early Childhood Unit looking at enhanced communication with children under three through the use of everyday stories of their lives. The 'Everyday Stories' data can be accessed through the National Children's Bureau website (www.ncb.org.uk). There is an evaluation framework for looking more closely at your interactions between children and adults and also those between children and children. The idea of 'telling a child's story' is used in the Babywatch study in Chapter 6 in which you can read all about Ellie's day at her children's centre nursery and how the staff members listened to and tuned in to her. Such stories can be used reflectively with staff members to allow them to look more objectively at their practice and focus on aspects that they would like to improve on.

Listening to babies

Listening to babies helps them to feel valued and know that their needs are being responded to. Indeed, *not* listening to the distress cries from babies can actually lead to more aggressive behaviour and anxiety later on. From the earliest stage, most adults who care for babies enjoy 'listening' to their vocalizations, their behaviour and their responses so that they come to know the baby well and to tune into what is important to that baby. The first step is to tune into the many different ways in which babies respond to their worlds and to see how these responses can be interpreted as communications. Adults who are tuned in to babies can identify their different cries, know what will stimulate and interest them, follow what babies are looking at so they can talk about this, interpret the sounds and actions that babies make and offer calm support throughout.

Another way of improving our communication with babies and making sure that it is a two-way process is through the introduction of baby signing (see resources). As with many Sure Start services, Stockton-on-Tees has been developing the use of baby signing as part of the regular work carried out in 'Stay and play' groups with parents and carers. The use of signing makes the spoken word easier to understand by babies and can also, through the signs that babies and young children begin to use, clarify what a young child is communicating to the listener.

In Newcastle City, a project on improving young children's participation revealed that at many community events, there was little to involve or interest babies and they spent most of their time sitting in their buggies. A 'Baby Tent' was set up at such events to give them a safe space to get out of their pushchairs and explore. In Stockton-on-Tees we developed a 'Babywatch' technique as a reflective exercise for staff on how they might listen to the babies in their care more attentively – there are more details about this in Chapter 6.

Communicating through a hundred languages: Reggio-Emilia

In Italy, there is a method of 'going with the child' known as the Reggio-Emilia approach. Because each child's way of learning is valued and developed, a very inclusive approach becomes possible. The central concept is the 'rich' child – a child rich in potential and competence and closely connected to the adults and children around. The child is seen as autonomously capable of making meaning from experience, and it is the adult's role to activate this in the child. Activities are built around the individual child's interests as they develop and reflect on their ideas and what they have learned. Each adult holds respect for the 'hundred languages' the child is felt to have been born with and each child is provided with the opportunity to express themselves and learn in as many different media. This inclusive approach is able to provide each child with a sense of belonging to family, school and community and with a positive view of their self-worth, whatever their needs.

A listening culture

If you have decided to take 'listening to young children' on board and to look at ways of changing your policies and practice to embrace an improved listening culture, then why not use listening itself as part of this process? For example, Lambeth Early Years and Sure Start Service is keen to develop a culture of listening to children and is pioneering various approaches to consult children and young people. In 'The Listening Group', for example, parents and carers are seen as the experts in listening to children and are brought together with early years professionals to devise approaches for consulting with children.

Chapter Three

Participation is for everybody

Some interesting work on participation has come out of the thought that no-one knows better what children want and need than the children themselves. Whilst practitioners are duty-bound to have clear views about how they will deliver the EYFS curriculum, do they always take the time to take on board the children's views? Listening to children and learning from what they have to say can be invaluable when planning a truly inclusive curriculum that enables each and every child to participate and to learn. Here are some simple methods that can be used.

Using cameras

With younger children, you can gather them in small groups of two or three and talk about what the best thing in the setting is. This helps them to focus their thoughts and share ideas in the company of friends, which can be less intimidating for some children than being asked one-to-one. Using digital cameras the children can take photographs of their most important or 'best' things. When these are downloaded and printed off, they can serve as further talking points about what the children feel about the setting and their daily activities.

You might be surprised by the photographs that the children choose to take. You might have supposed that your main attraction was the expensive climbing frame that you invested in last year, but many of the children might actually value the dark corner beside the shed where they can play hide-and-seek and make dens! Many practitioners who have used this kind of approach have come to realise just how important the outdoors is to young children and this has affected policy decisions to create more outdoor spaces for children to play in. There are some examples of this in Chapter 5.

Children can use their photographs in other ways too. They can be used to present choices to the children about what they would like to do. They can also be posted into boxes with a happy/sad face to indicate activities that they like and ones they are not so keen on. You will read about an example of how the children used photographs to make their own children's prospectus in Chapter 7 in 'Molly's Day'.

Child conferencing

You can also use small groups of three or four children to ask prepared questions about the setting and your activities. This is suitable for slightly older children who are willing and ready to talk and discuss things together. Make it clear that children do not have to take part if they do not want to and that there are no 'right' or 'wrong' answers. Everything the children have to say should be valued.

Observations

Use your regular observations (perhaps with photography as well) to monitor the children as they select activities and initiate play. You can learn a great deal about how involved and engrossed children are in their play and note some of the more complex links and associations that children are developing as they combine one area of play with another. Children's learning rarely fits the neat boxes that adults like to define! Your notes and photographic 'audits' of how equipment, areas and activities are regularly used can also be a useful tool in deciding which to adapt or replace in order to present that aspect of the EYFS in a more appealing way to the children.

Using displays

As mentioned in the previous chapter, Lambeth Early Years and Sure Start Service is keen to develop a culture of listening to children and is pioneering various approaches to consult children and young people. In 'Our Lives in Lambeth', children up to the age of six have been asked to send in photographs that illustrate their lives in Lambeth, to be used in a touring exhibition. These act as talking points for other children and adults and can stimulate all kinds of ideas and comments from whole families which are useful for building into the planning procedures.

Chapter Four

Tuning in to young children

Getting to know children as individuals

As soon as you get to know children as individuals, you reach a point where listening can truly begin. Though obvious, this point is sometimes more difficult to reach than we might suppose. We work with whole groups of children using frameworks that have been prescribed for everyone and we like to make sure that children are fully included within the group. Yet at the same time, we need to begin to form a relationship with each child as an individual, so that the children feel secure and confident enough to express their feelings and their views to us. Getting to know children as individuals also allows us to tune in to what they are thinking and feeling more closely, through our observations and day-to-day lives with them. When a child comes new to a setting, we might need to look for methods which allow us to get to know a child as quickly as possible. This allows us to make sure that their first days are happy and successful and also allows us to 'start where the child is at' in term of the experiences we offer.

All about me

There is a useful pamphlet 'All about Me!' that forms part of the PEAL (Parents, Early Years and Learning) training materials (see page 43). Within it, there are pages for a parent or carer to enter names and photographs of important people in the child's life, important things that staff members should know about the child – 'things I like to do at nursery, things I don't enjoy at nursery, things that make me happy about starting school and things that make me worried'.

Child passports

Whilst it should be easy to tune in to children who can tell us their views and feelings, it can be more of a challenge to tune in to babies, or children who have complex disabilities. You will find an example of how to tune into babies in 'Babywatch' in Chapter 6. One way of helping colleagues to tune into children who have severe and complex needs and who may not be able to communicate with you clearly is to develop a 'child passport' for them. The organisation 'Kidzaware' has produced one worth looking at and there is also information available through SCOPE. There are pages on friends and family, about me, nursery and hobbies, the 'physical stuff' (any special equipment and aids needed), communication, eating and drinking, 'medical stuff' (for example, allergies, any advice on seizures, managing asthma and medication), contact numbers and action in emergencies.

The communication section can stand on its own if a child's disabilities are such that it is difficult for those unfamiliar with a child (such as new staff members, baby sitters, other parents etc.) to understand how the child makes his or her needs known. In the Stockton-on-Tees Portage Service, one family put together a 'Communication Book' for their child. This is laminated for easy handling and can hang from the wheelchair wherever the child goes. As an example, these are some of the pages it contains. Each page contains one of the statements below and a matching photograph of Oscar which clearly illustrates the point.

Each photograph has a unique combination of expressions, body language and even facial colouring (for example, the first gentle blush of sleepiness) that signifies to the experts (Mum and Dad) what is going on. By asking the family to share a picture of these with an accompanying text saying what Oscar is feeling in each photograph and what someone should do about it, Oscar can then communicate his needs quickly to those who are just beginning to become acquainted with him.

Welcome profiles

We might also use child-centred questionnaires or interviews that a parent or carer completes when their child first joins the setting. Open-ended questioning such as 'Tell me a favourite toy/activity/family outing/memory . . .'; 'Is there anything which makes your child particularly worried?'; 'How much help does she need when going to the toilet?'; or 'How does he let you know when he is cross/happy/upset?' allows the practitioner to gather honest information about all children regardless of their ability. Some settings have involved the children in designing and illustrating these to make an attractive document to share with new parents and carers.

Chapter Five

Offering young children choices

There are two strands to offering choices in order to encourage participation and involve the children. The first is to be conscious of offering children regular and real choices in the day-to-day activities in your setting, both planned and unplanned. The other is to offer choices and seek views in a genuine attempt to consult the children on something that affects them, such as a new play area or even a development within their local community. In this chapter, we will look at both of these.

Sharing the menu

When offering choices to children, it is important to realise that children will go for what they know. In the interests of offering wider choices, it is important to think about how to introduce children to what is 'on the menu' so that they can make genuine choices – if swings and roundabouts were never available in public spaces, children would not know to ask for them, let alone to choose between them. Another thing to remember is that you cannot always ask young children direct questions and expect direct answers. Being asked 'What do you like?' in a discussion group may yield very little, but taking children on a walk and showing them real and concrete choices stimulates plenty of ideas and comments. Moreover, the results you obtain will depend on the way in which you ask the questions, who you are and your relationship with the children. You cannot obtain young children's views straight away to prescription – it takes time and space. Participation is therefore not an 'add-on' but something we should actively believe in and build into our everyday work and play with all the children. Participation through offering choices also involves a real flexibility on the part of staff. There is no point in consulting the children if you are not prepared to change and develop in the light of your findings. It takes a level of staff confidence to be able to do this!

The Mosaic Approach

How can children's views and experiences become the focus for reviewing services? The Mosaic Approach (see page 43) is a multi-method approach in which children's own photographs, tours and maps can be joined to talking and observing in order to gain a deeper understanding of the children's perspectives on their early childhood settings. As a first stage, children and adults gather documentation together using observations of the children, child conferencing, cameras, tours, mapping, role play and finally parents', practitioners' and researchers' perspectives in order to form a 'living picture' of what it is like for a child being in a particular place. The child conferencing is done very flexibly using a broad framework of questions, but acknowledging that some children might not wish or be able to answer. For example 'Why do you come to nursery?'; 'What do you like best?'; 'What part of the nursery don't you like?' Because each and every child is different, the mosaic of approaches is needed so that everyone can participate in their own way. As a second stage, the pieces of the mosaic are brought together with an emphasis on different pieces of the mosaic depending on whether or not a child was verbal. Themes begin to emerge at this stage such as children valuing 'places to hide' or 'playing with friends'. These allow practitioners to listen to and take on board the children's own perspectives about their setting.

Consulting young children about the room layout

There is no point in asking children about how to set up a new nursery room prior to it being opened since young children usually need concrete experiences in order to express their views. You can design and stock it based on what you already know to be important to the children, perhaps involving the children in looking through catalogues or visiting other settings. Once you are up and running, it can be a fascinating project to spend a few days simply asking the children about rearranging the room and trying out new arrangements. You might be able to observe real changes in the way the space and equipment are used that reflect the new and more involved ways in which the children are playing. Even by simply offering disposable cameras to the children you can observe which areas are photographed more than others. Is there one area that is underused or undervalued? What can be done about this?

Consultation with children about Sure Start services

In one Sure Start service in the north east (North Moor in Newcastle), consultation took place to ensure that the children's voices were heard during the development of new satellite sites. Children in local playgroups were given disposable cameras with which to take photographs of their likes and dislikes. Staff members also recorded the children's comments. A puppet or soft toy was used to encourage the children to talk and join in, and all the data was collected so that the children's views could be represented in the planning. Children came out firmly in favour of outdoor play spaces with a strong emphasis on being active and climbing. Balancing and climbing apparatus became the focus for prolonged imaginary play that the children liked to photograph and record. Bikes and scooters were popular playthings. Children took an interest in skies and boundaries as if exploring their personal spaces. The natural world also caught their attention. They enjoyed photographing displays of their work and creations and talking about them with a sense of pride.

Children appear to seek a balance between opportunities to be active and opportunities to be calm, being alone or being with a group and they enjoy a wide range of play and equipment. The researcher was also able to interview practitioners about the children's choices and preferences in their settings. This is an example of how, with a little extra time and attention, children's voices can be drawn into the process of community planning and, when the planners then listen and take note, have a real effect on the kind of provision planned for them.

Consulting with young children about where they live

The 'Walking with Children' project was coordinated by Sara Bryson, Listening to Young Children Officer for Newcastle City Council. Children between three and four years-old were given a say about their local area. They were taken on walks and invited to use photography, talk and actions to express their views. The main themes that emerged were that friendships and adult attachments were important to them. They liked nice gardens, open grassy spaces and had a lot of ideas to contribute about traffic, how to use parks and play areas and the local shopping centres. They did not like rubbish, derelict housing, muddy areas and nettles, and made suggestions about the general tidiness of the area. Each finding from the project was linked to a recommendation for planners to consider, thus ensuring that the children's voices had a direct input into the planning and development of their area. A dissemination event allowed the children to see the results of the project and allowed adults concerned to pledge their continued commitment to listen to the voices of children.

Consulting with young children about their local park area

Children in the Ropner Park area of Stockton-on-Tees were fully involved in the design of a new park area through the organisation 'Friends of Ropner Park'. A sub-committee of children and young people were given the remit of making suggestions for a play area and events to cater for children under five. Through the creative initiative of local childminders and parents, groups of children were taken on visits to explore other play areas so that they could express their views. They made sure that young children with disabilities were included and that there were opportunities to try out equipment suitable for their needs. Art work showing all the children's views and ideas was collected and displayed in the local school. Children were particularly drawn to some equipment around a ship theme which led to the design of a play area that had real value and use to local families.

Chapter Six

Tuning in to babies: Babywatch

Whilst most of us can visualise how we might listen to and involve older children more closely in what we do together, it is more challenging for us to think about listening to babies. This chapter looks at one approach which allows practitioners to reflect on the babies in their care and how they can participate more fully.

When it comes to babies, we can make sure that they are fully involved by considering these four strands:

- *Communicating effectively* – babies communicate all the time through their sounds, movements, actions and signals. Do we 'hear' and respond to these whenever appropriate?

- *Encouraging participation* – our role becomes one of making sure that all can participate in what we have to offer. Do we offer a broad and balanced session in the context of the EYFS? Do we help each baby to take part and feel successful?

- *Tuning in* – are we good at tuning in to babies as individuals, recognising and interpreting their early communication? Can anyone do this, or does it take a key person who knows the baby well?

- *Offering choices* – do we understand that babies have their own priorities, interests, concerns and rights too? Do we offer choices so that each baby's individual needs and interests are met? In other words, how flexible are we able to be?

The 'Babywatch' approach is a method of using baby observations and the writing of a 'Baby's day' narrative to help staff members tune into the babies in their care as individuals and modify what they do to encourage more listening and participation. It involves three steps:

Step 1   A room leader, manager, outside support professional or independent observer (who is also an early years professional well acquainted with early child development) carries out a running observation of a baby's day or part day in the setting. Staff members do not know which baby is being observed, but do understand fully what the exercise is all about and feel positive about sharing what they do.

Step 2   This is written up as a narrative story describing the day through the eyes of the baby, if only the baby could talk. All names are changed and the interactions are jumbled up so that individual staff members and interactions cannot be easily identified, unless it is by the person concerned who remembers the detail. This makes it easier to share the observation later in an unthreatening way.

Step 3 Staff members then reflect on the narrative using a structured feedback session. They discuss how they would like to modify their behaviour in order to encourage better listening and fuller participation.

We have reproduced a section of the observation below and also the feedback session in full detail so that you can consider adapting this method as an exercise in reflective practice at any age level. This activity was carried out by staff members at Footsteps Nursery, Billingham and the names of child and staff members have been changed to protect their anonymity.

Here is an extract from Ellie's day reproduced with permission from staff members who took part in a 'Babywatch' observation. This will allow you to see how the observation led into the reflection discussion during the follow up session.

Ellie's day

09.00
Hello – my name is Ellie. I have settled into the baby room of my nursery day and most of the babies have arrived now. I toddle up to the water tray on the floor, put my fingers in and watch my helper, Jenny. 'You want to climb in, Ellie, don't you!' she says and we smile at each other. I spend a few moments watching the other children around the tray and reach for the large, plastic spade. Now, after a careful toddle around the edge . . . I'm in the water! Jenny smiles – 'You're in now!' I grin all over my face. Of course, my dress is very wet now but no-one minds. It's warm in here.

09.15
I toddle to the low table with the play dough on it and poke my finger in. I decide that I like my neighbour's piece as well and collect both pieces up, squashing them. My neighbour doesn't mind as he's happy with the tool that he is exploring and mouthing. Jenny moves in and shows me how to push the tool into the dough. She invites me to copy but I am more interested in watching the people at the moment. Gill says to Jenny, 'Yesterday she was putting it in her mouth but today she's playing with it!' They look pleased with me.

09.20
I love to pass small things to Jenny, watching her face, so that she can return them to me again. She takes time to do this with me. I toddle to the plastic toy shelf – I

can reach all the toys and choose. Zoe reaches over to wipe my nose as she talks to her colleague. I don't seem to mind but sometimes this makes me jump a bit.

09.50
Looking out the low window makes me want to babble. Beth says, 'What are you doing, Ellie? You can't go out with no clothes on!' I move to her and she passes me a toy. I am just beginning to explore it carefully when she rattles another noisily in front of me. I lose interest.

09.55
Jenny is getting the chunky little chairs out ready for a snack. I toddle over and climb into one all by myself. I even look for the safety strap and touch it, but I don't know how to do it up yet. I do know where it should go, but it doesn't seem to want to stay there by itself. I sit for a moment looking round the room. I wait patiently because I know the routines and feel content and settled with them. Someone moves in to strap me in.

10.00
We have our hands wiped. Jenny asks me first, 'Are you ready, Ellie?' and I hold my hands up. A plate is put in front of me with a slice of fruit. I pick up the orange and suck it. We suck and watch each other in silence. 'That was nice, Ellie' says Beth. I kick my legs and call 'Wawawa'. She replies, 'Yummy yummy'. 'Have you taken all the juice out of that one?' she asks and gives me some more.

10.10
I hold up my arms as Jenny lifts me out of my chair and places me on the mat. Up I get – my chair is still there and I just love to climb in and out of it. 'Are we going to do some <u>painting</u>?' asks Jenny. I like it when she makes the important word louder – I can only understand about one word at a time and this helps me realise what is coming next. I climb in and out of my chair happily.

10.20
I climb out and take a ride on the snail baby rocker. Beth asks me if I want my nappy changed. Off we go and she sings, 'One wet nappy . . .' as we go. She talks to me as she changes me. When I come back in, someone else is on 'my' baby rocker – you see, I haven't forgotten what I was just doing. 'Mine!' I say clearly. Jenny explains nicely that a friend is having a turn and distracts me with something else just as interesting.

10.25
Jenny shows me a plastic fire engine. She pushes it and makes a noise as I watch. A

friend takes it and I watch but do not object (you see, I'm learning!). I reach for another and move it long and we watch each other play. When the fire engine is free again, I move in to play with it.

10.40
Time to paint! I sit in my chair and have an apron put on me. I take a loaded brush from Jenny and make dabs and light strokes on the paper. It is slippy and Jenny has to hold all our pieces of paper down while we paint. I look at Jenny's face for her reaction but she is busy holding down paper and talking to colleagues. I dip my fingers in the paint and taste it – not good. I try adding dabs to my neighbour's painting too. We share. The sponge blocks are brought out. I like things coming out a bit at a time – I don't feel too overwhelmed with the selection but can still make choices. 'Dab dab dab' says Jenny as we print and squeeze the sponges.

10.50
I take my own apron off all by myself! Jenny moves in to wipe me. 'All done', she sings and talks gently to me. She helps me down but I don't want to leave my lovely chair so I climb back on. She shares a laugh and makes a game of this as she lifts me down yet again.

11.00
I move over to the large cushions where there is a large soft blanket. I lie down with my eyes wide open 'pretending' to be asleep. This makes me smile to myself. I manage to pull the blanket to hide my head and pop out again – what a pity – no-one there to play 'peep bo'! But I still play it anyway. I stand up and try to balance on the cushions as I walk in my bare toes. It's interesting to try to balance and it doesn't hurt when you bump down. I repeat the falling down bit because it is fun. I move from cushions to carpet to smooth floor, watching my toes as they walk.

11.05
I have found my shoes and socks. I gather them up. I spend several minutes holding a shoe against my foot but it doesn't seem to want to go on. I keep trying very patiently, watching it with interest. Then Zoe feels my back to check that I am warm and finds that I am fine. But then she gathers up my shoes to put them away. I am crestfallen! I cry out! Jenny explains to Zoe why I am upset.

12.20
Zoe puts me in a buggy and wheels me into the sleep corner. In your dreams! I am given a monkey toy to cuddle and explore it for a while but then lose interest. I twist and turn and try to see what's going on. I know I'm tired but I'm just too busy right now to

sleep. Can anybody hear me? Zoe wheels me to and fro in a rather lively manner which is quite interesting for a while. I decide I don't want monkey anymore. 'If you have a nap you'll feel so much better' says Zoe. But I wasn't feeling 'not better' in the first place – just yawning a bit. I'm far too busy to sleep today!

13.00

Everyone is getting ready to go outside. I can see Jenny outside putting out the toys ready for us all to go out there. I start to fret because I want to be there too. I try the door. It works and I'm out – only to be returned because they're not ready for us yet. I continue to try the handle and watch. 'Ah da!' I cry for 'outside!'.

13.15

And we're out. I look very happy indeed and toddle to the rocking bike. My friend wants one too so Jenny helps us to find one each. I rock with tremendous strength (for one who is still yawning!) Jenny puts on my socks for me. I move to watch a friend in the ball pool and pick up a ball to explore.

13.35

I rock on the rocker so wildly that I tumble off but Gill is there to pick me up and comfort me. 'Are you tired?' she asks. Jenny has another try at putting me in the pushchair but I use my reaction to tell her, 'No thank you' and, this time, I am listened to! Jenny points out that I have lost a sock and she passes it to me. I hold it against my other foot but notice that it already has a sock on it. That doesn't seem right. So I pull that sock off and hold the first one against my foot again. It still doesn't want to go on.

13.40

Jenny gently puts my socks on. I am happy to sit on her lap and have a quiet moment or two. But not for long – busy, busy, busy, and off I go . . .

The feedback session

During this session, the observer spends about 90 minutes with all room staff, leading them through a number of questions in order to help them reflect on the narrative. Staff members are given the narrative a week ahead so that they have the chance to read and consider it carefully. Here are the questions that might be asked, together with replies from our example of Ellie's day.

Activity 1 – 5 minutes

Each of you find something to read out to me that made you feel particularly proud of Ellie's day. Choose the best. Why did you choose it?

Here staff members selected passages that showed how Ellie's helpers had tuned into her love of water play and were flexible enough to remove her clothes ready for the inevitable! They also pointed out how quickly adults anticipated Ellie's needs and wants and moved close to support her. There were also repeated examples of how staff members approached Ellie and 'consulted' her before moving into a caring action – such as showing her the cloth and speaking before wiping her face.

Activity 2 – 5 minutes

Think about the communicating effectively/encouraging participation/tuning in/offering choices framework (see the beginning of this chapter): Is this a useful framework for looking at babies and participation? Why?

Staff members all felt that the framework was useful and could be used for training and for evaluation purposes, perhaps with a manager or room leader taking time to do a short observation and sharing the 'story' with colleagues. They felt that encouraging participation came into all that you did within a child's day and that each part of the framework could not exist without the others. The framework could also be used to evaluate how staff members felt they were doing at enabling the babies to participate fully.

Activity 3 – 10 minutes

Communicating effectively. Babies communicate all the time through their sounds, movement, actions and signals. Do we 'hear' and respond to these whenever appropriate? Highlight examples of ways in which Ellie communicated to you in all of these ways. What was the response of the adult each time? Don't worry about whether you feel it was a good response or not – simply observe what happened next.

Staff members were able to illustrate many ways in which Ellie used her voice, her movement, her actions and her signals to communicate with them. It was impressive how quickly she was 'listened to'. They noted that communication worked best when adults took a moment or two to observe and tune in to what Ellie was doing before stepping in and intervening. They also noted examples of Ellie communicating with the other babies.

Activity 4 – 5 minutes

Rest times for babies is a tricky issue! What did you feel about the examples in the script? How far should we 'listen to babies' and how far should we follow set routines? Reflect on this together and write down what your ideal would be.

Staff members felt that rest times always needed to be a balance between what parents and carers asked for and what the child appeared to need and want at the time. The observation made them think about how long to leave a baby who clearly did not wish to settle. They decided that each child was different as each had a different pattern of settling. They also felt that rest times should not be forced. They were justly proud of the way they collected individual information from carers on each baby's rest pattern and comforters. This would allow them to use personal comforters for each baby and decide how long to leave things before returning the baby to play and this is something they were now going to think about as a team.

Activity 5 – 10 minutes

Encouraging participation. Our role becomes one of making sure that all can participate in what we have to offer. Do we offer a broad and balanced session in the context of the EYFS? Do we help each baby to take part and feel successful? Look at the EYFS framework. Highlight evidence that Ellie enjoyed and participated in each area of this. Where do you feel your gaps are? List these.

Staff members considered the EYFS framework. They realised that, even though they might not have considered that they were 'doing' Problem Solving, Reasoning and Numeracy (etc.) they were laying all the right foundations in the range of opportunities they were providing and supporting. However, staff members identified some areas of play that they would like to see more of. One was sharing picture books based on the 'babies need books' approach. They also wanted to use more heuristic play materials and everyday home objects to supplement their bright and colourful plastic toys. They would have liked more structure out of doors to encourage a wider range of movement – cardboard boxes, covers to tunnel under and through etc. Staff members wondered about more use of graded light and light-reflecting things to look at and wonder at. For example, they might be able to use graded light in order to control arousal and to signal sleep areas.

Activity 6 – 5 minutes

Celebrate Ellie's success by each reading out one example of Ellie participating and feeling successful. Did it involve your response each time or could she also feel success in her own playing and in interacting with the other babies?

Staff members found many examples. They all agreed that Ellie had enjoyed a very successful day in baby terms. They noticed her looking very pleased with herself. They noticed her repeating actions that appealed to her. They also observed the positive way that adults responded to her, provided attention or joined in games that she had initiated. Finally they noted that the babies were enjoying each other and interacting successfully one with another.

Activity 7 – 5 minutes

Tuning in. Are we good at tuning in to babies as individuals, recognising and interpreting their early communication? Can anyone do this, or does it take a key person who knows the baby well? Each find one example of a successful 'tuning in' and one of not-so-successful tuning in. Do you feel the lack of success was not knowing the baby or not tuning in sensitively? All adults named in the script have been mixed up and their names changed, so try to handle this objectively and not personally.

There were constant examples of successful tuning in. Staff members quickly identified episodes that they would wish to change. One involved adults busy speaking to each other and missing a moment at which Ellie needed support. They also noted cover staff not reading signals that others would be able to. There were a few instants of adults approaching babies from behind and wiping/blowing noses etc. without 'negotiating' this with babies first. There was also one where Ellie was very focused on a pair of shoes which were promptly tidied up to her great distress! Staff members felt that observation was a very useful way to flag up these details and improve awareness of the issues.

Activity 8 – 5 minutes

How important is the key person's role here? How can she help colleagues to tune in better to the babies in her care? What is the role of parents and carers here? Write down workable suggestions.

In general, the interaction between adults and babies far outweighed those between adults since staff members knew each other so well as a team and had already worked out their routines and planning. They felt that it was very important to have the same consistent staff members working together with each other and the babies. They felt that gathering information from parents and carers was very important too. This enables staff to build up a file on each baby which each staff member was expected to read regularly and be familiar with. Staff members also reflected on whether you could 'learn' the skills of tuning in or whether some were more sensitive to babies' needs than others. They felt that it was a mixture and that this had implications for both training and selection.

Activity 9 – 5 minutes

Offering choices. Do we understand that babies have their own priorities, interests, concerns and rights too? Do we offer choices so that each baby's individual needs and interests are met? In other words, how flexible are we able to be?
Each find three things that were really important to Ellie. In the script, how did you change what you were doing in order to take account of her preferences?

Staff members noted and celebrated Ellie's interests in water play, in outdoor play, in shoes and in fitting herself into tight corners!

Activity 10 – 5 minutes

Were there any times when you felt Ellie could have, appropriately, been given more choices?

Staff members felt that Ellie could have been given more choice over sleep times. The observer also questioned the repeated interpretation of any crying or fretting as 'tiredness' and wondered if staff needed to help her interpret her feelings in a more sensitive way. Staff members felt that Ellie could have been engaged more creatively in the use of the musical instruments – perhaps developing reciprocal games and imitation.

Activity 11 – 15 minutes

Bringing it all together. Please consider each of the four focus areas and write together your ten top tips for encouraging babies participation for your colleagues. You can make this specific to your setting – your own 'wish list' for good practice.

Staff members decided on these ten ways to encourage baby participation:

1. Pause for a moment to observe before you interact.
2. Listen to the child's needs and what they want to do.
3. Follow the child's lead where appropriate.
4. Look at resources to make sure you can give the child adequate choice.
5. Extend on resources for particular Areas of Learning.
6. Extend visual stimulation at child's level.
7. Possibility of staff's increased understanding of child's individual sleep needs.
8. Celebrate child:child and child:adult interactions (over adult:adult).
9. Prepare and engage baby's attention before putting on bibs, aprons, etc.
10. Enjoy each other – that's why you chose this job!

Activity 12 – 5 minutes

Write down three things you will take away from this training exercise.

Staff members highlighted the following:

- Think before you act.
- Observation can be a really useful tool to help you tune in to babies.
- Make everything more child-focused.

Chapter Seven

Molly's Day: A Children's Prospectus

The National Children's Bureau has produced a really helpful series of leaflets, all downloadable from the internet. The series is called 'Listening as a way of life' and in one of them, Julie McLarnon writes about *Supporting parents and carers to listen: A guide for practitioners*. There is a very practical idea about supporting the children in a setting to produce their own children's prospectus. Parents and carers were encouraged to share this with new starters as part of the settling in programme for the setting. The booklet that the children produced contained a series of photographs about what the new children will find in the building and what will happen when they are there. There were photographs of where the children hang their coats, the toilets, where they wash their hands, the snacks and drinks available and the kind of activities that the children do there. This prospectus sends out a clear message that the children are important and that the setting belongs to them. The message to new parents and carers is that they are encouraged to share their child's experiences and enter into a dialogue about what happens in their daily lives there.

This was one of the ideas taken up in the Stockton-on-Tees Participation Project. The idea was introduced to the children at the Hartburn Nursery during group time. It was decided to involve a large puppet, Molly, in order to make the idea more realistic for the children as they then found it easy to think about all the interesting things that Molly would like to know, or ought to know, about their setting. Children took it in turns to call Molly over and show her what they were doing and used digital photographs to capture the moment. Sometimes the children wanted to take these photographs and sometimes they preferred an adult to, so that they could feature in the photographs themselves. The photographs were then shown to the children who decided on the final selection and what the words beneath them should say. Once approved by the children, the prospectus was easily assembled from the digital photographs and texts, forming an eight-sided A3 booklet with three photographs each side. The result was 'Molly's First Day at Hartburn Nursery'. Copies were given to each new starter and parents or carers were told that it had been put together by the children using their own words so that it could be shared with their child. A simple evaluation with new parents and carers asked how they used the booklet with their children and whether they all felt it was a good idea.

To illustrate this, here are some examples of what the children decided to say, each phrase carrying a selected photograph.

This is Molly arriving with her Nan.

Molly hangs her coat up.

We put our names in the box.

We sit on the carpet.

Do you like my sticking?

We like the sand. There's treasure here. The pirates got it.

We go to the toilet. We wash our hands.

We took a picture of Molly with our teacher.

We stand on the snake 'cos it's going in time --'cos we have to.

We play outside. We bring our bikes today.

We have a snack at the nursery. I like apple.

Lydia brought these biscuits from home to share.

Goodbye! See you all again tomorrow!

New families were asked what they thought of the prospectus. All parents and carers felt that it was useful to have something like this at home to talk about with their children and reinforce who the new faces were. Everyone liked the idea of having real photographs and some of the children arrived wanting to play with 'that baby' (this raises an interesting issue about using visiting Persona Dolls such as Molly – where is she when the children need her?). The new children enjoyed seeing friends in the photographs and this made the experience of joining the nursery seem already more familiar. The nursery concerned has now decided to develop its own version of the children's prospectus, built on the ideas of the children and using photographs and words taken and made up entirely by the *current* children.

The process was a learning experience for the author too because it brought home how listening and participation have to be a thread that pervades everything you do rather than a project to 'add on'. In an adult's enthusiasm to engage in an activity that encourages participation, it would be all too easy to impose that very agenda upon the children who, in fact, were perfectly busy (thank you) engaged in something else of their own choosing! There were several children in this activity who, quite rightly, said that they were too busy being pirates to play with Molly today! Nevertheless, early years practitioners are practical people who are inspired by practical tools and ideas and that this is a wonderful way, if you take your time and allow the children to develop their own ideas in their own time, to engage children and adults alike. A children's prospectus should be *by the children* and *for the children* and should focus on those features of the setting that are important to the children *themselves*.

Chapter Eight

Working with disability: Friendship matters

Another aspect of 'listening' that can seem challenging to early years practitioners is that of listening to young children who have disabilities. Their need to be listened to, to have their needs and wishes taken into account and to participate are as great as for any other child yet staff members sometimes find it harder to tune in and to communicate. 'Child passports' (page 19) and 'Welcome profiles' (page 20) are a useful way to get to know how a child with disability makes their needs known, especially when you are first getting to know each other. For example, you need to know as soon as possible how any child indicates a yes/no or like/dislike response. Objects of reference can be used to offer choices and observe the child look towards, behave differently towards, point to or reach for a desired object. Pictures and symbols can be used as choice boards in a similar way.

One important aspect of the participation project in Stockton-on-Tees was some work around friendships with children who have complex needs. Staff members at the High Flyers Early Support Nursery were asked to think about how they fostered friendships and child-to-child interactions in their classes. This enabled the author to observe them in action and 'bottle' the essence of what they did so that the ideas could be used to develop good practice elsewhere.

Friendships can be fostered through carefully managed meetings and greetings.

By welcoming the children individually to the room and then encouraging them to join their friends on the mat, staff members had opportunities to help the children greet each other. They used this social time to draw the children's attention to each other, to point out similarities and differences and speak as if the children were able to verbalise to one another. They always used names and took care to focus the children's attentions on their friends when talking about another child. When a child left the room (such as for physiotherapy), they took pains to encourage the group to say goodbye (a wave or a look) and, as a group, they celebrated the child's return together.

Know when to stand back.

There were many occasions when staff members noticed two children playing together happily, sharing the toys or playing creatively in the home corner. Though they celebrated this among themselves (showing that they saw this as a very important step) they did not interfere with what was clearly going very well for the children concerned. Thus staff members gave the child-to-child interactions both value and time. Classroom assistants in mainstream settings also need to set up these interactions and then have the confidence to stand back.

Tune in to the individual children.

Staff members knew that certain children found it difficult to play in a sociable manner or to sustain an interaction, so they also knew when not to stand back. For example, they would step in to teach the word 'gentle' or to interpret one child's wishes or needs to another. Their very presence at times allowed a positive interaction to carry on for much longer than it might have done otherwise, since they made sure that there was social turn-taking and a balanced exchange.

Therapy should be done inclusively wherever possible.

It is possible in most cases to carry out physiotherapy then and there on the play mat with friends all around. This gives it a much more natural feel and does not single the child out as having to be removed for specialist 'treatment'. Only if privacy or specialist equipment is needed does withdrawal become appropriate.

Friends are children we play with.

Research on how young children define their friends suggests that 'friends' are seen simply as those children with whom a child has spent time playing – nothing more complex at this stage. Therefore, if you plan opportunities for different combinations of children to play and share adult-led activities together, you can actually breed a sense of 'friendship' amongst the children. In settings where some of the children have SEN or disability, therefore, it is particularly important to set up activities that include all the children.

Targets for child-to-child interaction should be part of most children's IEPs.

This should be encouraged in mainstream settings as well as Early Support nurseries. Mainstream colleagues may not always recognise the early steps to friendship skills (such as simply sitting on a knee and watching other children, parallel play, then cooperative play) and may need to pay more attention to and celebrate the first signs of early friendship skills so that these can be built on.

Encouraging turn-taking games through adult-supported activity is an excellent way of teaching friendship skills.

Early support staff who outreach to mainstream settings often model how to do this as a practical way of encouraging mainstream colleagues to include the child socially. Early reciprocal games include rolling a ball between you, blowing bubbles for a child to pop and playing with musical instruments, leaving gaps for a child to respond.

Children's photographs are a powerful way of encouraging friendships.

Staff members used individual photo albums to catch children's interests in themselves and others, and to act as talking points. They used photographs at group time to mount on a felt board and to signal group membership. They used photographs to offer social choices ('who do you want to play with next?'). They also caught 'golden moments' on camera to celebrate with parents and carers and to talk through with the children themselves. All of these ideas would adapt beautifully to a mainstream inclusive setting.

Joint targets can be used to encourage friendships.

For example, a joint IEP might be drawn up so that staff members can work on two children learning to play together.

Visual helpers are so useful for children with Autistic Spectrum Disorder (ASD).

One strategy has proved very useful in signalling turn-taking on favourite equipment such as the computer. Staff members arranged for a small photo of the child to be attached to the computer to signal that it is that child's turn. When the turn is over, a picture of another child's face is attached, signalling that it is time for their turn now. You can also use huge sand timers or ringing cooker clocks to signal that in a few minutes time it will be time for something new. This helps children with ASD prepare for change.

Visual calendars also work well.

You can use photographs, pictures or symbols to create visual timetables. These can be adapted to include social choices as well – 'who I would like to play this activity with'.

Music circle time assists friendships.

A regular Music Makers or group circle time can be used to reinforce children's names, passing and receiving around the circle, greeting each other, etc. There is a range of friendship and sharing songs to go with this approach in *Music Makers: Music circle times to include everyone* (see page 43).

Routines and rituals provide the confidence to be social.

It was clear that the children responded well not only to routines, but to the rituals within those routines. For example, the familiar ritual of the photographs and the felt board at group time (above) allowed children to feel secure, anticipate what was coming next and even encourage each other to join in.

Some children may choose to be solitary.

We need to balance the need for some children with ASD to have solitary times with our need to teach them to be as social as possible. One possible solution is to have structured activity (such as sharing the train track) in a group, but to also allow a quiet corner for periods of stress reduction and solitary play.

Striking a balance.

There is a need to balance adult-child activity with child-child activity for children with complex needs. One solution is to suggest 'sandwiching' periods of the one with periods of free play (as in any well-planned nursery).

A new role for the support assistant – that of 'child magnet'!

There is always the danger that the role of PSAs in mainstream rooms becomes one of a shadow or someone who withdraws the child, and this can actually get in the way of a child with disability forming friendships. One huge advantage of having a new person in the room to act as PSA is that this person inevitably draws other children, eager to share experiences with the new adult. This can develop well into really interactive experiences since the PSA can then act as a bridge between the child with SEN and the rest of the group, interpreting the child's reactions or behaviour and helping the other children feel that they have socially connected with each other.

Each child, each PSA, and each mainstream setting is individual and unique.

Staff members spoke of the importance of matching any outreach advice to the particular situation. Perhaps 'recipe book' approaches about how to encourage children to make friends might not work in all cases. The kind of special needs support PSAs and mainstream colleagues always wanted, they felt, was practical information such as 'If this happens . . . then try this . . .'.

Resources

Books for adults

Alderson, P. and Morrow, V. (2004) *Ethics, social research and consulting with children and young people*. Ilford: Barnardos.
Tel: 020 8498 7844
Website: www.barnardos.org.uk/resources

Allen, T. (2004) *Accelerating Babies' Communication*. Stafford: QEd Publications.

Booth, T., Ainscow, M., Black-Hawkins, K., Vaughan, M. and Shaw, L. (2000) *Index for Inclusion: Developing learning and participation in schools*. Bristol: CSIE (Centre for Studies on Inclusive Education) in collaboration with Centre for Educational Needs, University of Manchester and Centre for Educational Research, Canterbury Christ Church University College.

Clark, A., Kjørholt A.T. and Moss, P. (Eds) (2005) *Beyond Listening: children's perspectives on early childhood services.*' Bristol: Policy Press.
Tel: 0117 331 4054
Website: www.policypress.org.uk

DfES (2001) *Learning to Listen: Core principles for the involvement of children and young people*. DfES Publications.
Tel: 0845 6022260 quoting ref CYPUCP1
Website: www.publications.teachernet.gov.uk

DfES (2001) *The Special Educational Needs Code of Practice*. Nottingham: DfES Publications.

DfES (2004) *Every Child Matters: Change for Children*. London: HMSO.

Early Childhood Forum. The *Listening as a way of life* leaflets can be downloaded.
Website: www.ncb.org.uk

- *Listening to babies* by Diana Rich.

- *Why and how we listen to young children* by Alison Clark.

- *Listening to young disabled children* by Mary Dickens.

- *Are equalities an issue? Finding out what children think* by Nicky Road.

- *Supporting parents and carers to listen: A guide for practitioners* by Julie McLarnon.

- *Listening and responding to young children's views on food* by Anne-Marie McAuliffe with Jane Lane.

Edwards, C., Gandani, L. and Forman, G. (Eds) (1998) *The Hundred Languages of Children: Reggio Emilia Approach – Advanced Reflections*. US: Ablex Publishing Corporation.

Kidzaware produce a *Pocket Passport* for children with special abilities.
Tel: 01924 385977
Website: www.specialabilities.co.uk

Lancaster, P. and Broadbent, V. (2003) *Listening to Young Children*. Maidenhead: Open University Press (McGraw Hill).
Website: www.coram.org.uk and www.mcgraw-hill.co.uk/openup

Lancaster, P. (2006) *RAMPS: a framework for listening to children*. London: Daycare Trust.
Tel: 020 7840 3350
Website: www.daycaretrust.org.uk

Mortimer, H. (2001) *The Observation and Assessment of Children in the Early Years*. Stafford: QEd Publications.

Mortimer, H. (2006) *Music Makers: Music circle times to include everyone*. Stafford: QEd Publications.

Murray, L. and Andrews, L. (2005) *The Social Baby: Understanding Babies' Communication from Birth*. Richmond: The Children's Project.
Website: www.childrensproject.co.uk

The following are published by or available from the National Children's Bureau.
Tel: 0207 843 6029
Website:www.ncb.org.uk

- *Listening to young children: The Mosaic approach* by Alison Clark and Peter Moss.

- *Spaces to Play: More listening using the Mosaic approach* by Alison Clark and Peter Moss.

- The *Parents, Early Years and Learning* (PEAL) materials by Helen Wheeler, Joyce Connor and colleagues, published by the National Children's Bureau (2006) in association with Coram Family, Camden and Sure Start.

The following are all published by Save the Children.
Tel: 020 7012 6400
Website: www.savethechildren.org.uk

- *Never too young: How young children can take responsibility and make decisions* by Judy Miller.

- *Starting with Choice: Inclusive Strategies for consulting young children*

- *Journey of Discovery: Children's creative participation in planning* by Judy Miller.

- *Young Children's Rights* by Priscilla Alderson.

- *Participation Spice It Up!* by Carol Sheppard and Phil Treseder.

- *Empowering children and young people* by Lina Fajerman and Phil Treseder.

- *Children are service users too* by Lina Fajerman and Phil Treseder.

- *Children as partners in planners* by Fajerman et al.

SCOPE: For resources relating to children an adults who have cerebral palsy, contact www.scope.org.uk

Tiny Talk Baby Signing & DVD
Website: www.tinytalk.co.uk

The following are published by UNESCO.
Helpdesk: 0870 606 3377
Website: www.unesco.org/publishing

- *Creating better cities with children and youth: A manual for participation* by David Driskell.

- *Children's Rights & Responsibilities* – a leaflet containing a summary of the United Nations Convention on the Rights of the Child.

Books to share with children

Books to encourage talking and listening around feelings:

- *The Best-Loved Bear* by Diana Noonan and Elizabeth Fuller (Scholastic).

- *Scared of a Bear* by Hilda Offen (Hodder Children's Books).

- *No Worries!* by Marcia Williams (Walker Books).

- *The Good Mood Hunt* by Hiawyn Oram and Joanne Partis (Oxford University Press).

- *Hug* by Jez Alborough (Walker Books).

- *I Love Hugs* by Lara Jones (Scholastic).

For books reflecting differently-abled people visit www.diseed.org.uk (Resources).